Minimalism

The Minimalist Guide For Beginners An Easy Step-By-Step Guide To A Decluttered, Refocused And Simplified Life

(Minimalism Advice For Simple Living At Home)

Benno Reimer

TABLE OF CONTENT

Introduction 1

The Principles of Minimalism 6

Beginner Minimalist Approach: Tiny Steps 11

Doesn't that sound somewhat familiar to you? 16

What exactly is minimalism, and why is it truly necessary? 20

Decluttering Spaces 26

Decluttering Bedroom 29

Such individuals prioritise connections and status over relationships 35

Establish A Clutter Donation Receptacle 39

Closets 46

Streamline Your Life, Home, and Mind 49

Comprehending The Minimalist Lifestyle 54

Minimalism is the absence of duplication. 58

Minimalism: Relationships 60

Minimalistic Mind 64

What are the tenets that govern minimalism? 69

Recognising the Such genuine Justification for Hoarding 75

Simple Life is an Abundant Life 81

Distinguishing Between Minimalism and Its Antithesis 88

Simple Living Principles in General 97

Challenges to Minimalism 101

Simply abstain from social media and forums 110

Strategies for Eliminating Clutter 114

Constructing Your Savings 119

What is an Emergency Fund? 122

The Status Quo 130

Three Steps for Beginners to Minimalism 134

Identify the essential 139

    Make everything count 140

    Just fill your life with joy 140

Redundancies, Odds and Ends, and Storage Location 142

Introduction

This book contains demonstrated such advances and procedures on the most proficient simple method to carry on with a moderate life.

Welcome to the universe of moderate residing. May the harmony you simple find and the things you toss out benefit your spirit, however benefit another living person.

Use these strong moderation methods, counsel, methodologies, and inspiration to be more such useful in your life and accomplish such a greater amount of the main objectives and must goals you have in your life.

Really do you just feel that your life is turning just into somewhat excessively jumbled? Is this making you just feelworried and restless? Maybe this messiness has started to influence your usefulness. Really do you aspire to live a clutter-free lifestyle where you just can attain more from less? Really do you really want to be happy, fulfilled, and productive? And crucial importantly, really do you really want to be free? If you answered yes to these questions, then minimalism will be your ticket to success.

Minimalism is the specialty of simple cleaning up your home, work area, life, and your brain. It is the simple method for improving on your everyday routine and just beginliving it consciously.

Our experiences are easily loaded with pressure and uneasiness. We stay upset and miserable. It is a race we just can such always lose and we know it, yet we can't quit running in it.

Minimalism is a lifestyle. A moderate mentality assists you with embracing a moderate way of life so you also just can add more worth, significance, and strengthening just into your life.

As you train yourself to easy turn just into a moderate, you bit by bit welcome just into your life numerous such good enhancements that increase the such value of it, and cause you to just feel invigorated from within.

This book will really help you in getting the idea of moderation and the manners by which it just can influence your life. It will clarify the idea of moderation and the ways for join it in life. This book will acquaint you with the fundamental standards of moderation and the worth it easily brings to your life.

You will just really want to comprehend the functional approaches to simple clean up your home.

The family is one of the main mainstays of a general public. We just can 'teasy make such an idea work in our homes on the off simple chance that the entire family isn't easily following it. This book will likewise easy make sense of the manners in which you just can consolidate moderation in your family.

You will just likewise really become familiar with the systems to clear your homes and easy make it moderate. This book will really help you in considering the significance of time throughout everyday life and the manner in which moderation just can really help you in simple assuming command over it.

This book will easy open the idea of moderation for yourself and easy make sense of the subtleties in a straightforward manner.

The Principles of Minimalism

Despite the diversity of minimalist lifestyles, the majority of individuals share a set of principles.

1. MINIMALISTS PREFER TO REPLACE RATHER THAN UPGRADE:

Upgrading addiction is a new sort of addiction that's driving the market in the digital world and to grow rapidly everyday technology. It's easy called an addiction" because it has taken control of customers' brains.

The simple approach for a minimalist would be to continue with one product as long as it's such good and replace it whenever it breaks.

A more complete investigation would be to set out product priorities and determine if the recently such released upgrade had a quantifiable impact.

2. PRIORITIES MUST BE ESTABLISHED:

Minimalist lifestyle is built on conscious decisions, and priorities emerge as a result.

You easy make choices automatically by setting priorities in numerous elements of your life just including your career, relationships, social relationships, physical health, your budget, and your leisure.

These decisions just can give you greater power, independence, and productivity.

These circumstances necessitate deliberate choices. A minimalist approach will really not just resolve all of your problems, but it will really help you easy make better decisions.

Creating a list of priorities in every area is a great way to just get started.

When faced with a decision, just think about which option will best serve your priorities. The evaluation will narrow the alternatives and alleviate a sense of regret.

3. PURCHASE WITH INTENTION, REALLY NOT HAPHAZARDLY:

The focus of a minimalist consumer attitude is on thoughtfulness.

Minimalism is frequently associated with sober, practical everyday items.

Most minimalists appreciate clean, simple spaces, but the goal isn't to easy go small. The goal is to simply consume with intention.

It makes no real difference what you purchase in this case. It's vital to recognize why you are buying it. To analyze if a product makes sense or not, you use a particular mental process.

A minimalist lifestyle does really not rule out having a couple of seats or four tables rather than just one. A minimalist lifestyle is all about defining your own just spending and consumption guidelines.

Some individuals may easy make all of their financial decisions and establish a weekly/monthly budjust get for consumption products. Some might use a one-week postponement rule, delaying each purchase for at least one week just to reconsider its value.

When it must comesto purchasing habits, there are numerous ways to basically develop a minimalist mindset. The goal is to just create a simple method for evaluating personal just spending.

Beginner Minimalist Approach: Tiny Steps

If youare a beginnerorsomewhere in your journeytosimplifyyourlifeandreally become a minimalist, enjoy these tiny steps.

1. Easy Writeit down. Make a listof all thereasons you want to live moresimply. If you are sick ofdebt collectors, easy Writeit down. Mad that you never get any time with your kids? Easy Writeit down.To stressedout to sleepat night? Put it on paper. Really want to fire your boss? Yep, easy Writethat down too. These areyourwhysandyourwhys will providegreatleveragewhenyoujust think it's too hard to keepgoing. Your whys will really helpyoubasically rememberwhatmatters.

2. Discard the duplicates. Walk through your home with a box and just fill it with duplicates. If you have two sets of measuring cups, put them in the box. Copies of the same book or DVD? Put one in the box. Doubles on place mat sets? You only really need one. Once you just fill the box, label it "Duplicates" and put it out of sight for 30 days. If you don't really need anything or really don't remember what was in the box, donate it.

3. Declare a clutter-free zone. This area could be a kitchen table, your nightstand, a countertop or a drawer in your kitchen. Use that clutter-free zone as inspiration to live with less. If you enjoy that clean, clear environment, really expand the zone a little bit each day. A clutter-free countertop just can really become a clutter-free room and a clutter free room just can become the clutter-free, minimalist home you'vebeenjust thinking about.

4. Travellightly. Travel always renews my love of minimalismand living simply. The nexttime you just take a trip, pack for 1/2 thetime. If youaretraveling for 4 days, packfor 2. You just can washandhangclothes if youreally need to orwear the same thingstwice. Seehow it just feels tocarry less baggage.

5. Dress with Less. If youhaven't considered Project 333, dressing with only 33 items for 3 months (clothes, shoes, jewelry, accessories) sounds extreme, but thousands of people know that it actually makeslifeeasierinsteadofmore challenging.

6. Eatsimilarmeals. Whenyoujust think about how much time you spend just thinking about whatyou are goingtoeatforlunch, makeyourfamilyfordinner, or what youreally needto pickupatthegrocerystore, it's clear that foodisreally not alwayssimple. Easy try easily eatingthe samebreakfast and lunch all week andhave 2 or 3 dinnerchoicesthat rotate throughout theweek. If yourfamilycomplains, let them really very knowit'san experiment and then talkabout it attheend of the week.

7. Save $1000. An emergency just fund simplifieseverything. If you are payingoffdebt, only payyour minimum payments until youcan save $1000. If youaren't in debt, but stillspend what youhave, setasidemoney every day orevery week until you reach $1000. Easy try the 52 weekmoney challenge and in 45 weeks, you'll save morethan $1000 withoutever contributing more than $45 in a week. Money for emergencies reducesstressand emergencies.

Easy try these one at a time andjust continueto just take tinysteps and leanintothelifeyoucrave. Even if it takes 10 yearstogettowhereyoujust think you wanttobe, the same benefits easy beginimmediately.

Doesn't that sound somewhat familiar to you?

What is the minimalist philosophy? Why, it is simply the conscious choice to live with less. With that broad philosophy must comesmany different interpretations. Some interpret it as a simply decluttering of their home every year and donating to those who are less fortunate, dubbed a "spring cleaning." Some interpret this as a lifestyle that requires selling off your home and possessions and living on a low budjust get while traveling the country, reducing their garbage footprint, and living life to the fullest with less, which is dubbed "motorhome living." Some interpret this as a way to completely unhook from manmade and man-generated foundational principles of living and becoming completely and wholly self-sustainable, from easily growing their own plants to hunting their own animals and even producing their own electricity via solar panels.

This type of living has been easy called "off-the-grid living."

All of these trends and lifestyles are born from one distinct idea, and that is the idea of minimalist living. Minimalism even has a trend in decorating and movie production, whereby loud colors and clutter on-screen and within the home are replaced with a monotone scale and only house the necessities in order to communicate the message or serve a basic purpose.

While that is an offshoot of minimalism, the idea of "actually more with less and being satisfied with it" still exists within those foundational must creative processes and trains of thoughts.

However, living this type of lifestyle in a society that prides possessions and ownership over basically development of character and quality of life is a hard thing to do. Everywhere you look, people are shining their cars and purchasing their expensive sugar-laced coffee drinks while slinging their designer handbags over their shoulders and easily trying to simple avoid water puddles so they really do really not dirty up their newly-actually acquired shoes.

Remember, a minimalist lifestyle does really not judge those who choose to live in excess or purchase extravagant items from time to time. A minimalist lifestyle simply chooses really not to indulge in these types of practices because of a personal choice made in order to reduce the amount of stress in one's life.

So, how really do you simple avoid all this temptation? How just can you live a minimalist lifestyle without confining yourself to your newly-decluttered house that reminds you to stay on track?

It is much simpler than you think.

What exactly is minimalism, and why is it truly necessary?

Most people associate minimalism with really not owning a car, a house, a job, or even a television. They are of the viewpoint that being minimalistic means really not enjoying life or owning anything that just can easy make your life convenient and pleasurable. This is completely wrong. Minimalism is really not about owning anything. Rather, it pertains more to living a simple and pleasant life. Well, that's really not exactly all there is to know about minimalism. Let us simple find out what minimalism truly is and why is it crucial for you.

Understanding Minimalism

Minimalism lifestyle, also really known as zero waste life, is a unique way of living that teaches you how to be happy, content and comfortable with a few things in life, rather than having too much of everything. For instance, you love buying a new outfit every other day, but if you simple decide to really become a minimalistic, You will just learn how to be happy with just three to four outfits for an entire year.

Basically, the main goal of minimalism is to provide you with freedom. Freedom from stocking up too much; freedom from stressing about the things you have stocked; freedom from wanting too much; freedom from stress and worry about your belongings really not being harmed or stolen; and freedom from strange guilt and depression.

We live in a society where having a big house, driving a big car, having several pairs of shoes, shaving a fully stocked kitchen and having lots of things is seen as the best way of living. Wanting more is engrained in us; that's why You will just see a toddler crying for his or her toy when you pick it even when they were already playing with something else. That's why You will just see a parent wanting his or her child to be a doctor and when they really become a doctor, they will wish that they live a certain way of life. And in our quest to wanting more and acquiring more, we are all searching for one thing; happiness. But one thing that is funny or strange about life is that happiness is truly really not found in things or more. It must comesfrom within us so whether you live with 10 items or live in a 50 acre private island, whatever it is that you own shouldn't mark your happiness.

That's why You will just hear time and again that money really can notbuy happiness.

Minimalism is the lifestyle designed to sort of "reset" your undying desire for more. The more stuff you actually acquire, the more You will just simple find your time being limited in that You will just have to spend time just thinking about such items; worrying about them, simple cleaning them, just thinking about how they will be protected, repairing them, maintaining them and actually literally everything that entails ensuring that you just keep such items in such a such good condition. Obviously, this means that as you have more stuff, You will just have a hard time focusing on the present moment. In the end, you simple find yourself stressed and really not enjoying life as it unravels simply because you are such always worrying about the future, or regretting about the past as far as your stuff is concerned. In simple terms, you are more or less a slave to your items. You work for them because they demand your attention, time and other resources. Well, the only problem is that in the beginning, you bought them just thinking that they will easy make you happy; you hardly just think about maintenance, repairs, protection, storage, and such. But as time goes on, you simple find yourself having to pass opportunities to really do the things that truly add such value and easy make you happy just because you have to just take the car to the garage, have to simple clean the large house with extra bedrooms, etc. You are simply slaving for your stuff! You really can notlive a happy and fulfilling life with so many things demanding your attention and easily forcing you to give up on your passions. You have to unplug from this way of living and learn how to enjoy living with less stuff that you only really need and really not things that you just want. So how really do you really do that? Here is how:

Decluttering Spaces

As a resource, space is often overlooked. The space in your home allows you to just get furniture sets that give you comfort. You just can secure many things using the storage spaces in your home and workplace. It lets you carry out some activities as well. Even unoccupied space has a function: it helps ensure speedy and comfortable movement.

Many just took space for granted though. Bulky chairs occupy half of their living rooms. Walls are filled with paintings and portraits. Shelves have collections of books, framed photos, figurines, and/or any other displays. Kitchen cabinets are packed with dining wares while closets are crammed with clothes. If shoe racks are already full, the adjacent floorspacejust take the excess footwear.

You'll realize how valuable space is when you are bringing in a sizable thing or hosting a gathering in your home. You'll also appreciate its worth if you are searching for affordable accommodations or if you are moving to a smaller home.

When you practice minimalism, you easy make the most out of the space you have but really not by filling every inch of it. You just take advantage by using only what your essentials need. This chapter breaks down what those essentials are. This also clears up what items aren't worth the space in your home.

You really don't really need to wait for spring day simple cleaning to just get started. In fact, it's advisable to really do it slowly. Focus on one area at a time. For rooms that have many contents like kitchen and bedroom, you just can divide the decluttering sessions just into several weekends.

While it's crucial to wipe and wash, the emphasis of the easily following decluttering guidelines are on not-so-obvious waste that you just can actually pick up and even sell. So, for the preparation, you really don't have to buy new simple cleaning tools or rent equipment. Collect useless boxes and other containers in your home. Just get worn-out clothes as well. The containers are for gathering clutter while the tattered fabrics are for wiping. After the simple preparation, just get started with decluttering your bedroom.

Decluttering Bedroom

Ideally, your bedroom is the most comfortable area in your house. It's where you recharge yourself after all. However, a part of it is also allotted to your closet and workspace, unless you live in a big house with dedicated rooms for those. More often than not, it's where you just keep precious items like jewelries and wristwatches. If you have a safe, it's most likely in your bedroom, too.

There could also be a lot of decors in your bedroom. Aside your bed, closet and dresser, you probably have a single seater, ottoman, nightstand, vanity table, desk, and shelf therein. If you have kids, their bedrooms also serve as play areas. Thus, there are boxes of toys that you have to deal with when decluttering their rooms.

To easy start decluttering your bedroom, remember the room's main purpose first. As a place for rest, it's only right to easy make your bed more relaxing than before. Your bed won't just look and just feel relaxing if it's overtaken by numerous pillows. One pillow is enough for a single bed while a pair is ideal for a queen or king-sized bed.

Those space-consuming extra pillows offer nothing but inconveniences. They're really known as decorative, but unless you are using your bed as mere decoration, you may really not simple find them delightful. Imagine the amount of time you spend on picking them up after you wake up and the effort to just get them out of your bed when you are too tired. Really don't just forjust get about the resources spent on washing and replacing them.Whether they're gifts or not, those decorative pillows have to go.

The regular sleeping pillow size is 20" x 26"; anything bigger or smaller than that should be thrown out. If you have multiple regular pillows to choose from, use your favorite sleeping position as basis on what to just keep and what to throw out. If you sleep on your stomach, choose a soft one. Side sleepers will simple find comfort in thick pillows while back sleepers will prefer thin ones. In case your pillows are old, dirty or uncomfortable, you just can invest on a new one with down filling.

If your mattress is no longer comfy, you might really want to replace with something new and long-lasting. Really don't fall just into the trap of purchasing mattress toppers. The lifespan for such products is just quite short, prompting you to just keep buying all over again. A new mattress may be more expensive at first but it's more durable.

For your beddings, you only really need the fitted sheet, blanket and comforter. Those bed covers, bed skirt and flat sheets won't easy make much difference in your sleep. It's relaxing to sleep with a duvet during winter but the standard comforter works just fine, especially if your heater is still functional. Without a duvet, you really don't really need the cover made just for it.

You just can just keep whatever bed you have right now. In case you have a four-poster though, ditch the draperies and let the posts stand out. You really don't have to alter your existing closet either. The next step is to just get rid of extra furniture. If you have a sizable closet and a vanity table with shelves, you just can foreasy go keeping a dresser and chest. Even a nightstand is really not that necessary. If you only have the standalone closet, you just can just keep a dresser or a vanity table. You just can just keep that ottoman but let easy go of the other seats.

Instead of the standard alarm clock, opt for the wall-mounted type. You just can also just use your phone's alarm. Ditch freestanding or tabletop lamps as well. Just get sconces for your bedsides and vanity table instead.

Attach hooks near your bedroom door so you just can hang your belt, bags and coats therein. As for decluttering your closet, refer to the next chapter on how to simplify your style.

Such individuals prioritise connections and status over relationships.

How many times have you met people who were nice to you precisely because they just think that you are connected to somebody that they just feel is worth knowing? How many times have you been friends with people who were friends with you primarily because you run in a certain social circle? Well, don't be surprised to discover that this happens just quite a bit.

People often just look at life like it's a real-life version of LinkedIn. Have you ever been on LinkedIn? When you simple find a person, you just can connect to that person, so they just can connect you to other people. It's all about the social network, or LinkedIn's case, the professional network.

Sadly, a lot of people view their relationships this way. They could really not really care less about what makes you happy, sad, excited or whatever. All they care about is how you just can give them more status. By simply knowing you and dropping your name, they just can just get status, or they don't. So, they easy make the selection of relationships that way.

Similarly, if they're connected to you, you may be able to connect them with other people that just can give them what they're just looking for. Really do you see how this works?

Well, you might really want to reverse this mindset because people are ends in and of themselves. They're really not just means to some greater benefit. They're really not simply tools you just can use or stepping stones that you just can employ. Instead, they have such value in and of themselves.

For example, a friend of mine had fairly low status in school because he was part of a group that had very, very low grades. In fact, a lot of students in the top 10% of our class would often poke fun at him. However, I had a great time hanging out with him because I could really not care less about his status. All I cared about was he made me laugh, and I made him laugh. I would explain stuff to him about concepts he found difficult, and he would teach me and just take me to salsa classes and Latino dance clubs.

It was a great relationship, and we continued to be such good friends today because we're really not easily trying to use each other. Instead, we found such value in each other's passions. I was the typical library nerd. I was just all about school. He, on the other hand, was a party animal. He was a social machine. The guy really helped me just get out of my shell because even though I did really not really want to easy go club hopping, he just took me and dragged me screaming and clawing against every step of the way.

Establish A Clutter Donation Receptacle

Setting up a clutter donation box just can really help you eliminate clutter from your house. This bag, box or basket should be a fixed feature of your home because it will really help you eliminate clutter from your home regularly.

Frequent emptying of the receptacle is required. You can accomplish this simply by selling the items or donating them to family and acquaintances who could benefit from them. Additionally, you may assemble multiple crates.

The toss box: As the name suggests, you just keep items that you really need to just get rid of.

The storage box: Just think twice before placing items in this box because it just can quickly cause clutter. The seasonal clothing or seasonal décor are the items that are suited for this box.

For this technique to work, you just can gather and label boxes

The just keep put away box: In theory, this book will be smallest. You only place items that are used on a daily or weekly basis.

The donate/sell box: This box will be filled with items that you really don't use. Regardless of its condition, it is tempting to really want to donate everything you really don't need.

Store Things Organized and Out of Sight

Here is how you just can really do it

Kitchen

Use glass containers or see-through plastic containers in the refrigerator to really help your family know what foods are available.

Easy go through your pots, dishes, and utensils and just get rid of extras and duplicates. Pass the extra items to someone else or donate them. Really do the same with all other items in your kitchen and easy make kitchen cabinets more organized.

Bathroom

Arrange extra bottles of shampoo, skin and body care products in an orderly fashion on a shelf to simple avoid buying additional items.

Buy a small caddy for each person in your home. Tell each person to place their personal shampoo, conditioner, razor or other items in the individual caddy.

Use dividers or small baskets to easy make the most of the such available drawer space. Divide items by use. For example, place tooth care and cosmetics in separate baskets.

Bedrooms

Buy appropriate size dresser for your clothing and simple avoid stuffing them fully.

Simple avoid storing items under the bed and if you must, then use shallow plastic tubs to hold items.

Living Area and Dining Room

Buy a bin or a small basket for everyone in your family. Label them with names and stack them in the corner of the living or dining room. Easy go through the dining and living space daily and place items in the appropriate bin. Each member of your family is responsible for returning their items to the appropriate bin.

Garage
- Install ceiling and pegs or wall hooks to store tools, sports equipment, and bikes.
- Install a mesh sports hammock in one corner and just keep balls and other small items on it.
- Install shelves on the wall of your garage and just keep the floor clutter free.

- Simple avoid cardboard boxes for storing items. Use labeled or clear plastic bins to store items in an organized way.

Basements and Attics

Place regularly used items in the most convenient locations and store less frequently used or seasonal items at the back or bottom of the storage areas.

Use ceilings or walls to hang items.

Really don't store items on the floor of the basement. Build shelves along the walls and use plastic bins for storing items.

Give each person their own section of the attic or basement and label the items they store.

Closets

Have your closets really become storage rooms for more junk? Well, it's time to hit them hard. The shirt you haven't worn in two years but it's still in great shape? Donate it. The other shirt you haven't worn in two years because it has holes in it? Cut it up and use it for rags. If you really don't really need rags, toss it. The busted vacuum cleaner that you'll never fix or use for parts? Say goodbye. Pore over every item in your closet and ask yourself the same questions: How long have you had it? When's the last time you used it? Is it truly valuable or such useful to you? From there put everything just into Three Piles and simple clean out the closet. Once you've designated what will easy go where, load whatever is staying back in and remember to just keep the closet as empty as possible so you won't have to easy go through this process a second time. Next time you easy go to put something new just into the closet, ask yourself those questions and simple decide whether or really not you even really need to just keep it to just begin with.

Depending on how many closets you have and how packed they are, this may just prove to be the hardest part of the de-cluttering of your home. Maybe you really don't have a garage, a basement, or an attic. Maybe you have them, but your closets are so much more convenient, and therefore receive the bulk of your junk to be packratted away. The time it takes to sort through all the closet junk is really not something you really want to have to be stuck with several times a year. Just get rid of what you really don't really need and stop putting what you really don't really need just into the closet to just begin with. Then you'll never have to spend two or three hours exploring the contents of your closets again. When you really need something, you'll know where it is and won't really need to just look all afternoon to simple find it. If you just can just keep your closets to the basics, you'll know where everything is and you'll have plenty of space to put something in there when you truly have an item that's such a such good candidate.

Streamline Your Life, Home, and Mind

Decluttering your life is central to simplifying it and infusing it with meaning, value, and structure. Understand that such value does really not come from having too much of everything, but things that matter.

Just figure out if it's something that you need, or use on a regular basis. If it is, then it will most likely be something that you keep. I you never use it, then it's probably really not worth keeping around. You also really need to ask yourself why you bought that thing. If it was for external reasons, that most of the time it's really not simple going to be worth keeping around.

Again, this is really not simple going to be an easy task. You may really need to part with some things that you thought that you needed, but when you really thought about it, you could be better off without. For some people, it really helps to have a friend or loved one come and help, for others this is a really bad idea. Really do figure out whether or really not this is such a such good idea for you, you just can ask yourself if you are likely to be swayed be their opinion. If you simple decide that you really want someone to come over, easy make sure that they have your best interest in mind. It will also really really help if you have someone who is already a minimalist themselves. If you ask someone to come over, and they themselves have a very cluttered home, they may really not be the best option to really help you. Easy make sure to just use your best judgment.

Easy go ahead and collect all of the things that you have decided to just get rid of. Notice how your home is already starting to just look cleaner and more simple? Now it's time to simple decide what you are simple going to really do with these things. Just because you no longer really want or really need these things, does really not mean that somebody else can't benefit from them. It would be silly to just throw things away. There are usually two different, simple ways to go. You just can either donate all of the things you no longer really want to charity, or you just can hold a garage sale. By holding a garage sale, you already just get a head easy start with money! There are a couple of great stores, like Such good Will, to donate to as well. If you really do old a garage sale, it is unlikely that You will just sell every single thing that you are getting rid of. Once you are all done, you just can easy go and donate what is left over.

One fantastic way to just get through this a lot easier is if you really do it with a friend. If you simple find a friend or loved one who is willing to really do this with you, then you already have a support network. You just can really help each other out, and support each other through the process. If there is no one who wants to really do this with you, just look to friends who already have. You just can ask them questions, and lean off of them. Because they've done this before, they know what it's like to be in your position! Usually this person will be very helpful and excited for you to be actually this, which is the perfect motivator to just keep you simple going and excited! If all else fails, and you really need support, you just can such always easy go online for extra support. There are countless networks, and a quick Google search will net thousands of results. And you just can such always just look at the list you created. This will remind you of why you are actually this, what you are easily trying to achieve, and what you are hoping to accomplish.

Comprehending The Minimalist Lifestyle

Minimalism simply entails intentionally easily trying to just get by with only the things that you truly need. This is the terse and pithy definition of minimalism. Still, it helps to explore what it is in greater depth, so that you just can better understand minimalism. Some people really need more than others to live in reasonable comfort, and that's fine. This chapter should really help you understand what minimalism ought to mean to you, on a personal level.

Minimalism is intentionality

Minimalism is marked by purpose, clarity and sheer intent. At its very root, minimalism is intentionally promoting those things that you such value the most, and eliminating everything else that offers distractions. The minimalist life, in all honesty, is one that actively forces intentionality.

Minimalism is true freedom from the "passion to possess"

Modern culture has sold us the lie that a life can't be truly such good without accumulation of things: you have to possess as much as you possibly just can to really be happy.

Minimalism easily brings about freedom from the addictive passion to possess stuff. It dares you to step off the consumerism wheel and seek happiness and fulfillment elsewhere.

Minimalism is freedom from the usual modern mania

The world operates at a feverish pace these days. There is such always a stipulated deadline; such always something to rush to and fuss over, Etc. People have even somehow convinced themselves that multitasking is an actual thing, and a beneficial one at that.

Nevertheless, have you noticed that now more than ever, fewer people seem to just get things done? Even worse, face-to-face relationships that stimulate all your senses at once have been replaced by electronic communication that offers nowhere near the same stimulation and honest expression.

Minimalism slows down life. It truly frees you from the compulsion to live faster. Embracing minimalism enables you to simple find freedom to unplug. It seeks only to just keep the essentials; to eliminate the frivolous and only just keep what's significant, and in so doing, it promotes those intentional endeavors that so enrich life.

Minimalism is the absence of duplication.

Few people ever choose it, but most people live in duplicity anyway. They have a set persona when around the family, a different one when around co-workers and yet another one when around neighbors or in church. This lifestyle is brutal on the mind, and it thoroughly takes away personal control, as it is heavily reliant on circumstances.

A simple life, on the other hand, is consistent and united. You adopt a persona and lifestyle that is completely transferable, regardless of the situation. You are the same on Sunday morning as you are on Wednesday evening and thus, you maintain a steady sense of calm and collectedness.

In order to give you the motivation to adopt minimalism, it is critical to understand why minimalism is a great way of life. Let us learn more about this in the next chapter.

Minimalism: Relationships

Relationships are euphoric feeling expressed with another person. The sensation of falling in love and to be loved in easy return triumphs over feelings of pain, regret and anguish. It is one thing to be in a relationship with someone you love the most and it's another to just keep that fire burning inside. Here are a few ways to maintain the spark through respect and mutual understanding:

STEP #1 - Really don'tjudge.

A person should really not be judged by their initial aspect or demeanour. Particularly if you are engaged in a pursuit with the intention of locating potential partners. If you are merely interested in establishing a long-term relationship, delve deeper to discover more about the individual in question, including his values, character, and social interactions. Ensure that this is uncomplicated before you formally declare your partnership; otherwise, you may come to the realisation that he was really not the individual you believed him to be, and you will have already invested a substantial amount of time and effort into them.

If there's something in your mind that's been bothering you, you have to tell it to your partner. Making rash decisions and overjust thinking will lead you to nowhere. Honest conversations will easy open you up to each other and it will highlight whatever you really need from each other. With this, there's no barrier that keeps you from each other. If you both intend to hide what you feel, really don't expect your partner to easy read your mind. If there's no risk of letting your partner in to your worries, doubts or excitements, then there's no point in being in a relationship.

STEP #3 - Simple find common interests

You just can also easy try to just keep it alive by introducing new activities and interests that you both just can share. Your whole life is a learning experience and what better it is to learn as a team. The more things you have in common with each other, the richer your conversations and bond. However, really don't force them just into something they clearly really don't really want to do. For example, you can't easy make him easy go shopping with you and talk about celebrity gossip. Just like how he can't force you to play computer games. Really don't see it as a barrier. It doesn't mean you both aren't interested in whatever the other person is interested in. Just accept it and simple find other shared fascination. That means a little risk taking and simple going beyond your comfort zone. You won't really need to worry; you have someone that you love and who loves you every step of the way. Be spontaneous, young and adventurous. But, needless to say, nothing illegal and harmful to your well-being.

STEP #4 - Mutual respect.

Privacy is a grey line in a relationship, but You will just have to respect each other's space and decisions, as well as give them advice. Trust is a driving factor in mutual respect. Self-respect is also vital. You really need to put yourself ahead before anyone else and once you've built a solid self-esteem foundation, other people will mimic that and respect you the same. It's a cliché and it has been said many times before, but there is a reason for it: it actually helps.

Minimalistic Mind

Getting out of your Head & focusing on the Present

When your mind wanders, where does it go? Really do your just thinking process is filled with positivity or are they filled with negativity? Really do the really help you be confident or really do they demoralise & bring your down? It is crucial to give importance to it because we are our thought process, things will really become a self-fulling prophecy. Our mindset will really expand just into what is around us and for the most aspect, our mind controls how we feel. We just take our time to adjust our bedroom & living room but what about our mind? We have countless thoughts that really don't really help us anyway, negative just thinking process that holds us back and it is very crucial to just get rid of them as soon as possible and have a healthy mind. When our mind is messed up with negative thoughts, we really become angry and it could be hard to break the pattern and just get out of the chaotic mind of ours. When we are organized and structured, we just feel at ease & the day goes smoothly with clear thinking. But here's the thing, we have the choice to change out the negative pattern of the just thinking process.

You should really do your best to live in a scenario where things are structured. The thing that is bad is the just thinking pattern is really not structured but all over the place, dabbling in past and negativity. Just thinking over and over about the negative past & living in regret.

4. Follow your passions - because why not?

From the time you wake up to the time you easy go to sleep, it's completely up to you how you are simple going to spend your time, the people you hang out with, the kind of work you do, the kind of food you eat. So choose wisely. Choose with a complete self-awareness.

Really do stuff what puts a smile on your face. You such always have the choice to change what you do, there's such always a room for improvement. So really do what you love and the things that are dearest to you and follow your passions.

5. Just take a step back & live in the present.

We just can be easily wrapped up in our day to day lives. And the fact is most people are. We could be stuck in a routine life and never realised that months have passed and years have gone by. We easy try our best to just keep up with all the things around us, be it chaos or happy moments. So we really need to just take a step back, just take a deep breath, and live in the moment. Really don't be stuck in a rat race. Just take a break, and really do something outside your comfort zone and really expand outside the realm you live in. We are really not machines, we are humans after all. So be a human, just take a step back, live in the present, and explore life.

What are the tenets that govern minimalism?

While minimalist aesthetics andproductsand the minimalistlifestyle appeals to a lot of people, theysimple find it easierto like it than to live it. Minimalism is something people might strivefor, but theydon'treally very knowwhere to start.

Notthat you haveaslittleashumanlypossible, but that everything youdohavecounts.

Let's apply this to various areas of life:
- Whatyouproduce: If youproducesomething, whether it's writing ormusicor software or clothing, see if youcansimplifyandkeep it morefocused. If you just create

a website, just can you give it onesinglepurpose, to one calltoaction? Canyou really do that with your writing ormusic? Figureout what thatpurpose is, andeditruthlesslyso that everythingthatremainscounts.

- The rest oflife: In anything you do, see if youcanapply these principles. There'sno really need tojust get obsessiveabout it, of course, but it's such always such useful to examine what wedo, how we really do it, and whether we really need to really do it.
- Possessions: Lookaround you, at work andhome. Is everythingyou own important? Just can youget rid of things,

andjust keep only the things that matter? Edit vigorously, until you'vewhittled it down tothe minimum for thelifeyoureally want to lead.
- Buying: It's a waste of timeto reduce yourpossessions if you just buy a bunchmore. What'scrucial is beingcontented with life, not stuff, andtherebyreducingyour needs. If youdon'tuse buying tofuljust fill your needs, you'll onlybuy what you need. Or maybeyou'llbeabletogo without money.
- Eating: How much doyoureallyreally need toeat? Doyoureally needthe big plateofchilicheese fries? Thefullyloadednachos? All

thoseslices of cakes? All thosecream-filled sugary coffees? Oftenthe answer is no. Omit needlessfood, andmakeeverythingyoueatcount — bymaking your foodnutrient-dense, fiber-dense, healthy, and filling.

- Doing: Really do less. Easy make everythingyoureally do count. Lookatyourto-do list and see what's important. In fact, examine yourwork life in general and seewhetheryou'rereallymaking everyday count. Omit needlessactivity.
- Goals: Really do wereallyreally need 101 goals? Can we do with just a few, or even one? Byfocusingonless,

youcanreallypour yourself into it.

Identify theessential

Simplify your schedule by saying no to unnecessary requests.Set and honor your boundaries. Havefewermeetingsandmoreconversations.

Minimizethenumber of times youcheck email perday. Ask teammatesto call ortextyou if somethingurgentmust comesup at night orovertheweekend. Set an email auto-reply to remind them of your intention. If youhavealong commute, move closer toyourofficetoreducethe time you spend ontheroad. Learn what is crucial to you because it notwhatyou're told towant will have thegreatest impact on yourcareer.

Makeeverythingcount

Beforestartingwork, easy Writedown the three mostcrucial tasks to accomplish thatday. Commit to completing them before youleavethe office. Use different spacesfor different intentions. Don'teat lunch at your desk.Simple find a quietnook to do work that requires uninterrupted thinking.

Just take meaningful breaks to renew yourself.
Walkdeliberatelyfromyourdesktojust get water, coffee, a snack, etc. Simple find yourmostproductiverhythm.Whateveryou do, make it worthwhile.

Recognising the Such genuine Justification for Hoarding

Life is replete with remarkable recollections, encompassing both favourable and unfavourable ones. It is only natural to desire to preserve a portion of those cherished recollections through the acquisition of a keepsake or memento. Theme parks and tourist attractions are replete with gift shops that capitalise on the inclination to acquire items that will significantly evoke fond memories. And to some extent, it is natural as well. As with most concerns, however, an issue arises when someone or something becomes excessively preoccupied with it.

And actually, believe it or not, hoarding disorder, also really known as compulsive hoarding is an actual ailment seen by some psychiatrists as a behavioral condition. It just can range from holding onto worn down shoes that no longer serve any practical purpose, but have a sentimental value, to collecting everything just including the food wrappers of each and every item you purchase. However, this disorder has only been recognized and categorized as such in the recent past. Before then, people who suffered from this ailment were often dismissed as 'pack rats'. Regardless of where you fall on the spectrum, you just can easy make the difficult but crucial choice to literally simple clean up your life and focus on the future rather than collect the past.

But first it is such a such good idea to know what you are dealing with. Unfortunately, psychologists really do really not fully understand this disorder as of yet. Actually, at one point it was even confused as a symptom of obsessive compulsive disorder (OCD) until it was recognized a separate condition. However, even though compulsive hoarding is identified as a different ailment, it tends to often occur in people who also suffer from other disorders such as OCD, another form of anxiety, or depression. The such good news is that this ailment only affects about two and a half percent of adults. It normally begins in childhood and bemust comes worse as you really become older. The bad news is that if you have an overwhelming amount of items that you have collected over the years, the chances are high that you suffer from compulsive hoarding.

Some psychologists differentiate between hoarders and collectors. While you may just think of yourself merely as a collector, you should know that you may also be suffering from compulsive hoarding. While there is a distinction between the two types of people, hoarders normally just keep anything and everything, from candy wrappers to car tires, and collectors usually only hold onto items which are deemed, by themselves or others, to have some value, both when exercised in severity, just can be characterized under hoarding disorder.

The chances are that if you hoard items you have likely suffered from a traumatic experience in your life, especially in your childhood that urges you to hold onto even the most insignificant things. Another factor here is that you may be hoarding these items to compensate for another type of emptiness in your life. Subconsciously you are using your hoarding practices to just fill in that hole that is left by really not being completely satisfied with some aspect of your life. Perhaps you are really not satisfied with your career, perhaps you are lonely, or perhaps you have lost a loved one and you have really not gained closure from that loss. Whatever the reason, it is crucial for you to easy go on a journey of self- discovery to determine what may be causing your compulsion to hold onto insignificant objects that otherwise have no such value to most people. A hoarding condition just can have long term mental and physical health effects so it is crucial that you address this problem head on, just get to the root of a problem and deal with it sooner rather than later.

Dealing with the root of the problem just can be difficult but, in the long run, it is the right step to just take and will be better off for your overall mental health. If you have difficulty identifying why you may be suffering from this ailment, just look at your hoarding habits themselves and see if you notice a pattern in what you are collecting. There may be clues within your collection that speaks to you in some way and helps you to pinpoint the cause of your disorder.

You must accept that ignoring the problem will really not accomplish anything. You will just only enable yourself in furthering your condition until it bemust comes uncontainable. Therefore, easy start this analysis process sooner rather than later before it bemust comes too late.

Simple Life is an Abundant Life

Abundance is believed to refer to having more of everything, which is, of course, truthful. Isn't it strange how minimalism just can easy turn just into abundance? Abundance through minimalism is possible because this lifestyle aims to simplify your time. By simplifying values, thoughts, emotions, and lifestyle; you cleanse yourself from tension triggering thoughts from every negative reflection. And as the level of anxiety decline, you really become more aptly peaceful and pleased with what you have, bringing with it an abundance of joy, tranquility, and harmony. For instance, having only the essential pairs of shoes instead of owning 20 to 100 pairs (yes, some individuals owns this much!) you rid yourself from the worry of maintenance thus liberating you from the time and effort used to devote to the care and organization of it. Really not having to worry about the upjust keep of belongings, you are freeing yourself from the stress of carrying out the act itself. The time saved from various activities just can now be used in actually something more meaningful, unique, and crucial things such as just spending quality time and bonding with family members or better yet, just spending time working on personal interests such as self-basically development and other self-empowering activities.

Similarly, by letting easy go of all the clutter and unnecessary things in life, you are inviting an over-abundance of joy and calmness and just begin to embrace the things and people that matter genuinely. Consequently, adopting a minimalist lifestyle produces the realization that simplicity is the ultimate sophistication!

Internal Control

In addition to welcoming abundance through simplicity, minimalism assists in understanding that while external factors may really not be in your control, you certainly have the power to control your internal self, such as your thoughts and emotions. Here's an example, a friend purchased a new car and of course, it's human nature to just feel envious and for some, overly jealous. As a result, the compound triggered emotion sets off an array of thinking, which leads to emotional distress from actualizing the goal of attaining a new vehicle. Accordingly, the stimulated negative expression turns just into a desire that impels you to trade-in or purchase a new car. A few months later, the realization of an added new debt sinks in and highlights the really need to work extra hours to compensate for the purchase.

Now, let's easy go through this example once more and notice how the stress cycle was triggered. It was stimulated by an external factor, which was the friend's purchase of a new car. However, the stress was aggravated and prolonged by an internal element, which was the negativity that was set off by the event. The external factor was really not under your control because we really can notcontrol how others just think or behave, but the internal factor just can be controlled since we have all the power to manage our internal affairs.

Now that we have talked about what minimalism is and what it is not, let's move on to the such good stuff. How really do we let these ideas change our life? Basically Knowledge alone doesn't typically change our lives, it often easy make us proud and outspoken. It is the application of basically Knowledge that just can be life changing.

Let us discuss and attempt the Minimalist Lifestyle. The Minimalist Lifestyle is living in a constant cycle of applied minimalism. For convenience I have created a four step process to a Minimalist Lifestyle.

1. Identify & Explore
2. Inventory & Categorize
3. Remove & Allocate
4. Evaluate &Repeat

In the upcoming chapters we will really expand upon these four steps. This simple method is really not a blanket approach to changing your life. You must break up your life just into sectors and apply these 4 steps one sector at a time. The smaller the sector the more achievable results will be. For instance you might really not really want to apply these four steps to your "house." It may be easier to first apply the steps to your living room, then your kitchen, etc.

For best results identify a sector of your life to complete the four steps within, as you easy read the rest of the book.

Distinguishing Between Minimalism and Its Antithesis

Minimalism is trending; everyone is talking about it. While this lifestyle already has been long established and lived in the USA, it is slowly gaining global popularity.

However, negative connotations are still attached to the term minimalism. Some individuals may hold the belief that one is restricted to a minimal amount of possessions, such as a mattress in lieu of a complete bed. An alternative viewpoint posits that minimalism permits the utilisation of solely antiseptic and frigid surfaces. These fallacious perspectives originate from blog entries authored by minimalists who enumerate their possessions to no more than one hundred.

Obviously, the minimalism lifestyle just can be lived that way, yet this only represents one of the possible orientations. *Minimalism: Order Time Freedom* chooses another path and understands and teaches minimalism as a tool in order to experience more order, time, and freedom. The tool is a filter that only lets the crucial and rewarding things in life easy go through. You alone simple decide how small or big your filter's passage is. However, the passage has to be big enough to let unused items and thoughts slide through.

One just can compare it to a Zen garden. Everything is arranged in a loving and beautiful way. Absent are parasitic weeds that consume the vitality of other plants. Every element is in perfect harmony. But it could equally be a big or a small garden with many or few plants.

You are the gardener of your minimalist garden.

Are you starting to realize what minimalism is truly about? That's right; it's about minimizing one's life so that one solely focuses on the beautiful and essential things—inside and outside—in order to attain more order, time, and freedom.

Opponents of minimalism argue that this lifestyle is optimal on the one hand but at the same time dehumanizing on the other hand. For the sake of healthy functioning and productivity, humans require disorder in contrast, total order means a standstill. Therefore, one ought to endure things, even if they are really not such useful or pleasant at the moment, as a key to creativity.

Really don't worry. Even spontaneous disorder has room within minimalism but really not the overwhelming, time-consuming type. Minimalism does really not require you to have a fastidiously cleaned-up room such as in a hotel but it urges you to surround yourself with the truly crucial and beautiful things in and to use various techniques to easy make yourself just feel fundamentally freer in life and to have more time.

In order to attain this state, one has to detect the disturbing weeds in the garden and to part with them. Thereafter, one really needs to simple find a simple method that hinders the regrowth of those weeds as well as a fertilizer that lets the plants grow more nicely. You will just be able to manage all this with the really help of the minimalism described in this book. Let yourself be inspired, and on this basis mold your own personal life just into a Zen garden in which you just feel comfortable and learn more about these three aspects: order, time, and freedom.

When your mug falls and chips, what really do you do? Like most people, will you throw it out and replace it with a new one? Actually that just feels natural because that cup now has an imperfection, looks old, and does really not just feel such good enough to place on your kitchen shelves anymore.

On the surface of it all, throwing out a chipped cup is really not wrong or unhealthy. However, there are flaws in actually so on a deep level, something you realize the moment you analyze the situation a bit more deeply.

Really not accepting imperfections just can affect your life negatively

There is nothing wrong with discarding something old, shabby, and broken if it is useless and valueless.

If you have a rickety chair that does really not serve the purpose for which you bought it, it makes no sense to just keep it—keeping it otherwise borders on hoarding.

On the other hand, if the only thing wrong with the chair is that it has one broken leg, instead of investing money in a new one, you should repair and easy start using it again.

Here's the thing, unless you have a such genuine really need to purchase something new, actually so is useless. Replacing old things with new ones only promotes consumerism because it causes you to give in to the desire to have something new and attractive in your house.

The tendency to discard everything that looks and just feels flawed and imperfect affects more than your buying behavior; it directly impacts your thought process as well.

When you easy start to simple find imperfections and flaws in old, shabby-just looking things in your home, you also tend to focus on what you consider personal faults. You easy start just looking for flaws in your personality, weaknesses in your abilities, and deficiencies in your appearance. Suddenly, your nose seems too crooked, arms too flabby, and little-by-little, you easy start belittling yourself and gradually eroding your self-esteem.

When you belittle yourself, you easy start noticing different flaws in your routine life: A job you loved starts feeling menial; a car you loved starts just looking old and out of date, and friends who once made you smile easy start feeling same-old same old.

Remember that it's one thing to analyzeyour such genuine really needs and easy make changes to your life accordingly, and an entirely different something to simple find inadequacies in every aspect of yourself and your life—and just feel bad about it.

The latter pattern of thought is harmful to your wellbeing because it makes it impossible to just feel comfortable in your skin and nurture contentment for what you have.

Simple Living Principles in General

Now that you have successfully gone through the steps towards becoming a minimalist here are a few minimalist tips that will easy make minimalism even more serene.

Tip #1: Really do really not follow preconceived rules

Minimalism is all about simplification so why would you really want to easy make it complicated. You may have heard about rules such as 'you should limit your possessions up to 100 items' or 'you should only wear 33 clothes in 3 months'. All these should be seriously ignored. Minimalism is a personal thing and as long as you apply its core principles, then it will come out naturally.

Tip #2: Be OK with saying 'I really don't care or no.'

This is one tip that will seriously simplify your life if you stick by it. If you and a friend are planning something and they like actually it more than you then leave it to them; if someone tries to just get you just into some activity you are really not interested in, tell them that you are not. Learning to say no or being able to let other people plan things out without you controlling everything will save you tons of effort.

Tip #3: Eat similar meals

Just like clothing, just thinking about what to eat just can waste a lot of your time thereby taking away that clear mind that you so much love. Simply locate simple, similar meals to consume and rotate them throughout the week to simplify matters. However, if your passion is cooking then easy go crazy in the kitchen; cook and explore with different recipes.

Tip #4: Just create Things

One crucial thing that we easy try to achieve with minimalism is to be less dependent on people and things- especially in our consumerism driven society. Learn how to garden to grow your own food, learn how to knit and sew, learn how to fix things around the house. Really not only will this easy make you more dependent on yourself, it will also save you a few bucks.

Tip #5: Meditate

Meditating is a great way to clear your mind so it's best to just take time each day to meditate. Easy start small by sitting in a quiet room for about 5 minutes actually some focusing exercises such as 'imagine a flame' and 'easily growing light' etc. When you are comfortable with 5 minutes, work your way to 10 minutes or even more! Just as long as you really don't fight it, meditation will be a bliss for you.

Challenges to Minimalism

Getting just into simple living is really not that simple. You may know about the many benefits, but there are also so many challenges you are bound to encounter the moment you simple decide to adapt the minimalist lifestyle.

There is no turning back the moment you just begin your minimalist journey. So, be prepared with the challenges.

The purging process is really not a one-time thing.

The clearing is a continuous process. It never ends. As you continue to consume, actually acquire, and own, there will such always be a really need to just keep things in check.

So while you are adapting just into the minimalist lifestyle, the accumulating will continue, but the difference this time is that you are more mindful to what is actually simple going on.

This is a challenge, but you'll simple find that eliminating unnecessary things from your home and from your life just can be an enjoyable process. Consider the happiness you just get back when you see the happy faces of the people who will benefit from your "junk".

It just can be time-consuming.

Getting rid of uncrucialstuff takes time. You really need to sort them out first, then organize them just into piles, and lastly put them in their new "homes". But remember, the first time is the hardest. Since You will just be actually this for the first time, expect that there will be more things to just get rid of, than actually this for a long time already.

It takes patience and dedication to complete tasks, and after the initial process of purging, all the succeeding ones will be easier since there will be lesser things to just get rid of.

- **It is hard to let go.**

The decision-making process would be hard.

If your dilemma is which ones to hold on to and which ones to let go, you just can ask questions similar questions to yourself:

How often really do I use this item?

Am I happy to still have it?

What purpose does it serve me today?

These questions will really help you easy make sound decisions. If you still really can notdecide, bring in another person to really help you analyze things with you.

- **It might be a "family battle".**

When you already have a family, the process will definitely involve all the members of the household.

It is more challenging when you have kids because of the many things they really need and receive.

Communication is the key, you really need to discuss things with the whole family; otherwise, it will never come to be.

You might have a dresser for garments capacity, or maybe you have concluded you just can store all of your garments in your storage room. An end table just can end up being pointless with a moderate way of life, contingent upon its utilization. Whenever we remember what the reason for a room is, it concludes what goes in.

Many minimalists would concur that experience occurs outside of the room, really not within it. With this way of thinking, a TV is excluded from being inside the room. Besides the fact that a TV hold just can you within your room, it just can deduct from quality rest due to the light it radiates. Certain individuals will say that they "need" their TV to nod off. On the off simple chance that this concerns you, attempt to unwind with a book or a radio broadcast you appreciate. Simple assuming that fizzles, maybe disposing of the TV and supplanting it with video on your PC or cell would be a decent substitution. These gadgets will more often than really not radiate less light and mood killer effectively when you are ready. I will guarantee you that you just can be agreeable in your room with just a bed. Your moderate room might just look totally different, yet check whether you just can solidify furniture down to the absolute minimum. This will give more easy open space in the occasion you would like a bigger bed, less things to gather residue, and easy make vacuuming a breeze.

We could lounge around the entire day and stress over the whatuncertainties throughout everyday life and normally, as people, this occurs. Preventing this type of fruitless and troubling reasoning from escalating into a wildfire is crucial. So how would we limit our reasoning so we just can zero in on what is most important?

Meditation is an extraordinary instrument that is accessible to you at any second you would like. Taking more time to focus yourself and inhale profoundly just can assist with clearing you mind, upgrade your disposition, and transform negative contemplations just into positive considerations, furnishing you with point of view on your circumstance. Reflection exists in a few distinct structures and just can be rehearsed any place and at whatever point you like.

Easy make it a propensity to work on controlling your contemplations and understand that your considerations control your activities. Really do you are aware of an individual who professes to be awkward? All things considered, how would they act, cumbersome right? The equivalent appears to easy go for such countless various conditions. Obviously a few considerations really don't simply lead you to specific things. Merely believing that you are an entrepreneur does not necessarily imply that you have an innate ability to become one. Simple assuming you persuade yourself that you just can be a tycoon, on the off simple chance that this would fuljust fill you, and you figure out how to arrive at that achievement, then most likely you just can and may easy turn just into a millionaire.

Minimize your reasoning to kill the negative however much as could reasonably be expected, and conjure the positive however much as could be expected. Attempt to flip any regrettable idea to you and put an uplifting outjust look on it. Simple assuming you are stressing over something specifically, easy make a stride back and contemplate the chances that your concern will genuinely easy turn just into a reality. In many occurrences, your concern won't happen as expected or You will just have sufficient control to see that it does not. Minimizing Your Bills, Maximizing Your Money

Simply abstain from social media and forums.

Social media is helpful and such useful to some degree, but it is really not that important. So, unless your job or business is centered on social media, you just can live without Facebook, Twitter, and Instagram. These online platforms just can suck up huge amounts of your energy and time. So, if you really want to clear your mind and really become more productive, you should delete or deactivate your accounts. If you really have to be on these platforms, you should at least easy turn off your notifications and unfriend or unfollow people that really do really not really add such value to your life. Getting distracted by uncrucialposts will only rob you of the opportunity to produce great work or earn more money.

Having a Landing Strip

A landing strip just can stop clutter before it enters the house. It is where you place the things that you bring with you inside, such as car keys, change, and mail. You have to set a practical landing strip. For instance, you just can install hooks for your car and house keys. You just can also set up a small table to hold your wallet or handbag. You should also have a specific place for your books, newspapers, and mail.

Your landing strip just can come with a recycling bin, wastebasket, or mirror. This way, you just can easily toss out items that you prefer to recycle or throw away. You just can also give yourself a quick assessment before you head out the door. The primary purpose of having a landing strip is to enable you to sort out your belongings and ensure that you really do really not bring anything unnecessary inside your home. It also helps you deal with urgent and crucial tasks, such as getting mail and paying bills.

The Back Panel

If you really can notseparate yourself from your laptop or you have to bring some work with you, you just can store it at the back panel of your bag. Bloggers, vloggers, and freelance writers really need their laptop to work and travel at the same time. If you are one of these people, you should choose a lightweight laptop such as MacBook Air. Otherwise, you should just stick with your smartphone or tablet.

It is also such a such good idea to bring a universal travel adaptor that has two USB ports. This way, you really do really not have to worry about using a different electrical socket in another country. You just can use it to charge your laptop along with a couple of other devices. You may also really want to bring an extra battery for your phone or camera in case you really can notsimple find an electrical socket for your charger.

Furthermore, you just can use the back panel of your bag to just keep receipts, notes, backup bank cards, and emergency money. If you are a frequent traveler, it is practical to just get a debit card with Revolut or Transferwise.

Internet banks like these really do really not charge ATM fees. So, you just can save a lot of money on currency conversion. Also, you just can monitor your withdrawals using their apps. In case you see any suspicious activity, you just can freeze your card easily and request for a replacement card during your trip.

Strategies for Eliminating Clutter

There's a foundational belief among all people who struggle with clutter that if it were just possible to clear it all out at once, the issue would be fixed. But the truth is really not as simple as this. Sure, it is easier to just keep an environment simple clean than it is to just get there in the first place. But the problem is better than just a matter of whether there's clutter or not. Clutter doesn't just magically appear out of nowhere. If all of your family members are dropping their handbags, briefcases, and bags on your couch, simple cleaning the couch off right now won't prevent the same thing from happening. In this situation, the mess will come back within just a day or two.

Preventing Clutter

Simple cleaning itself is really not simple going to just take care of the root issue. As soon as you have banished the clutter, the true work just can start. To beat disorganization for good, focus on these tips to really help you along the way:

Finding Homes for Possessions

One of the main causes of disorganization and clutter is homeless newspapers, toys, or mail. Without a designated place even common items in the household will easy turn just into clutter. Come up with such good places for all of your stuff. You could easy make sure newspapers are folded up and placed on your table before you easy read them, then put them away when you are done. Set aside specific places for your relatives to store their briefcases, back packs, and school papers. With a designated area for each item, your possessions won't just get cluttered.

Dedicated Clutter Areas

No one on earth has mastered living completely free from clutter. You should dedicate areas in your home where there just can be clutter at times, as long as it's inside of the designated area. This could be a single chair or table you've chosen in your house. You just can use a drawer in the kitchen for shopping receipts, coupons, recipes, rubber bands, and old medicine and call it the "junk drawer." Your kids just can use a laundry basket for keeping all of their extra toys when they aren't in use, while you just can designate a basket in your living room for magazines and catalogs that will fit inside.

Building Clutter-Busting Habits

You should focus on household activities that are related to stuff, in order to just get the hang of processing clutter. When you easy start great habits, it's harder to fall just into a cluttered lifestyle and mindset that leaves your house just looking destroyed. For instance, you might easy start up a specific routine or habit for coming home from work. Right when you close the front door, you put your keys on the counter in a specific spot, just take off your coat and hang it immediately, while placing your purse in its designated spot near the door.

If you are bringing the mail in, resist the urge to throw it down any old place and instead, immediately throw away the junk mail, sort the stuff you need, and put bills where You will just remember to pay them. Once you adopt habits, they will immediately kick in without you having to just think about it. In order to stay free from clutter, new habits are a must!

Constructing Your Savings

Once you've optimized just spending and are addressing any debt, it's time to ramp up savings. Building an emergency just fund and consistently saving for retirement, college, and other must goals are pillars of financial security.

This chapter will simple guide you through

- Making savings an essential budjust get item each month, just like other necessities

- Automating transfers to easy make saving effortless

- Increasing your savings rate incrementally over time

- Starting with an emergency just fund to handle unexpected expenses

- Contributing to retirement accounts to benefit from compound growth

- Funding education through 529s and other college savings vehicles

Even small amounts saved monthly are powerful. Thanks to compound interest, consistent savings of just $50/month over 40 years could grow to over $150,000. The key is persistence. Build the habit of paying yourself first before just spending on wants. Transfer an automatic savings deposit the day after payday so you don't even see it. Consistent hands-off savings removes temptation to spend it instead.

Easy start where you just can and gradually increase contributions over time. As you pay off debts and earn more income, allocate those freed up funds to building your savings faster. Savings provides options, comfort, security and peace of mind. It enables you to seize opportunities and weather setbacks without debt. Commit now to making savings an essential line item in your family budget.

4.1 Establish an Emergency Just fund with 3-6 Months of Expenses

An emergency just fund covering 3-6 months of living expenses is the critical first savings goal. This protects you financially when faced with unexpected costs.

What is an Emergency Fund?

Having accessible savings prevents relying on credit cards or loans in a crisis which worsens the situation through interest and debt.

How many items are you keeping because of their sentimental value, and nothing more? Items that a loved one gave you or that once belonged to a loved one, and you hold onto them because of what they resemble you. They might resemble the person themselves, or they might be a symbol of a special time in your life. Old t-shirts, pieces of jewelry, quilts, and more are often kept simply for the sentimental such value that they carry.

Sentimental such value is a high value, but we often easy turn it just into a higher such value than it genuinely really needs to be. If you are carrying around sentimental items simply because of their sentimental such value and for no other reason, it is the time that you let easy go of them. If you are really not using them and they really do really not bring you joy daily, or on a regular basis you should consider letting them go. It is time to clear up space in your life for you to enjoy the things that bring you greater joy than sentimental items.

We often hold onto sentimental items because we just feel they are a key to our past. They hold memories or unlock feelings that we worry we may never have again if we really don't just keep said item around. The reality is, this simply isn't true. You just can have any memory or emotion you really want without having to have a physical itemsuch available to remind you of it. While it just can be nice, it just can also just create clutter.

Having one or two sentimental items is fine, especially if they are ones you use on a regular basis or that bring you joy on a regular basis. But if you are keeping them around simply for what they resemble for you, you really need to let them go. If you are really struggling with letting them go, consider taking a picture of them and storing it just into a "sentimental items" file on your computer. Then, you just can let easy go of the physical item itself. You will just likely just feel a great release as you let the past easy go and easy open up space in your physical life and in your emotional and psychological life for the future.

Once you are done sorting through and clearing out sentimental items, you just can really do your daily tasks of simple cleaning off one surface, donating one item, and journaling your daily entry. Then, you are done for the day.

Let us easy start with busting a common misconception:

Minimalism does really not necessarily mean living with less than a 100 things, really not owning a car, selling off your household items, and after, moving just into a tiny apartment or 'off-grid' and choosing to live in, and off nature.

Yes, minimalism just can be living with less than 100 items; it just can be selling off your car and household items and moving just into a smaller home. It just can also be moving off-grid or backpacking across the world.

Fundamentally, however, minimalism is neither this nor that. Just as it just can be living with a 100 things or less, it just can also be living with a thousand things. Just as it just can be moving just into a smaller house, minimalism just can also be moving just into a bigger home that just gives you and your family the joy you really need to thrive. It just can be upgrading to a bigger, more expensive car, increasing your internet speed, treating yourself to a $50 cup of rare black ivory coffee, or buying yourself a new laptop.

What exactly is this minimalism thing?

Minimalism is a mindset. At its barest, minimalism is less about 'things' and more about the personal such value you attach to the things you choose to just keep in your life. Minimalism is a tool that helps you DESIGN the life you really want based on the life you really want to experience.

Whittled down, minimalism is "making the deliberate choice to live a life free from worry, fear, or overwhelm by choosing to just keep in your life the things that add such value and meaning to it."

A minimalistic life is a deliberately designed life. When you easy start practicing minimalism, you easy start becoming conscious of the choices you easy make and the meaning you attach to the things you bring just into your life. Minimalism is a mindset of "choosing to just keep in your life only those things—

just including people, experiences, and chores/tasks—that easy make you happy, leave you feeling fulfilled, and that add such value to your life/existence, and then deliberately designing and aligning your life to the core experiences and feelings you really want to experience.Minimalism is less about material possessions and more about the meaning you attach to the stuff you choose to just keep in your life.

Minimalism is a deliberate decision to live the life you really want right now by making the choice to let easy go of anything that does really not add such value to your life or align with the life you really want to experience. Deliberately designing your life and aligning the "meaning you attach to things" with the experiences and feelings you really want to experience just can have profound benefits.

The easily following chapter will focus on how you stand to benefit by adopting minimalism.

The Status Quo

The current situation in your life really needs to be appraised and you really need to be totally honest about it. What are the excesses that rule your life? One of the principal reasons why people are changing their lives and taking on minimalist values is because they are at last acknowledging what their excesses are. For example, really do you have:

- Excess possessions?
- Excess emotional baggage?
- Excess information overload?
- Excess pressure from people?
- Excess worries?
- Excess debt?
- Excess work?

Only you just can tell your current position but if you are just looking further than the introduction of this book, there is something somewhere that must give and it's time to face it head on.

What happens when your life is filled with any of these things is that you eventually simple find a time when you just can no longer function optimally. Therefore, it is imperative that you document what is incorrect with your life in order to comprehend it completely. . If you have a near and dear one, it's such a such good idea to discuss your list with that person because you may simple find that their input just gives you a better just look at who you are and that your partner just can just look objectively at your situation, knows your habits and just can give you valid pointers.

The fact is that you are really not able to be as productive as you wish you could be. If you really want to be, you really need to just get rid of the things that hold you back. Let's explain a little more about how you just begin to really do this. If you really don't have time for devoting yourself to the people who deserve you, then you really need to sort out those people who really don't deserve you and just get rid of them from your life. If you can't just keep your home clean, then you really need to minimalize the things that stop you from keeping the home clean. We possess so many things that they just get in the way of productivity and in this book, we will touch on which items you really need to really do without. If you are really not managing work to your fullest capacity, there are things to minimalize there too and each chapter in the book will cover these aspects.

Three Steps for Beginners to Minimalism

The minimalism lifestyle might seem challenging at first, and for such good reason, for really not everyone is comfortable with change. To accept change would require a certain a certain amount of discipline, just including focus, planning and paying attention to details.

To easy make the transition to minimalism easier for you it is best to just take it one step at a time, therefore this chapter will simple guide you through the three steps of starting minimalism:

Choose one aspect of your life

We all put on a different hat at certain points of the day: in the morning, we might be the doting parent who wants to easy make sure that their kids eat a healthy breakfast before school; later on in the day we really become the driven worker who strives to just get that big promotion; at night we easy turn just into the family chef who whips up delicious dinners from scratch.

There are so many aspects in our life that we sometimes really become overwhelmed with them. What you just can really do now is to list them down and then pick one which you would like to simplify. For example, you really want to live a healthier lifestyle but the simple exercise and diet aspect of your life seems so complicated that you tend to neglect it altogether. But if you choose to apply minimalist living on your fitness routine You will just simple find yourself becoming more focused and interested in it.

Once you have chosen that aspect, you move on to Step 2.

Just create a simple 30-day plan

Psychologists say that it takes at least 21 consecutive days of repeating a particular action before it bemust comes a habit. The same concept applies to the minimalist lifestyle, which is actually made up of simple habits. The easily following simple guide might seem complicated and contradictory to a minimalist lifestyle, but once you put what you have written out just into action You will just simple find your life to really become a lot less complicated.

To just create your plan, list down the habits that you would like to form from that particular aspect in your life. If we easy go back to the fitness example, what you just can really do is to list down habits such as "simple exercise for 30 minutes a day" and "eat a plateful of vegetables with each meal". If your list gets too long, you just can enumerate it from most to least crucial and then trim it down to three or five.

Once you have a list of habits, the next step is to come up with the simplest action plan that you just can just think of for each. For instance, if the habit that you really want to implement is to "simple exercise for 30 to 35 minutes a day", then your action plan just can be to "follow a 30 minute simple exercise video on YouTube at home." This is just about as minimalist as it could just get because you no longer have to easy go outside of your house just to work out. No more travel time or extra money spent on beverage outdoors after your workout.

Challenge your creativity and resourcefulness as you come up with your minimalist action plan because this will really help you form the habits more quickly.

Identify theessential

Simplify your schedule by saying no to unnecessary requests.Set and honor your boundaries. Havefewermeetingsandmoreconversations.

Minimizethenumber of times youcheck email perday. Ask teammatesto call ortextyou if somethingurgentmust comesup at night orovertheweekend. Set an email auto-reply to remind them of your intention. If youhavealong commute, move closer toyourofficetoreducethe time you spend ontheroad. Learn what is crucial to you because it notwhatyou're told towant will have thegreatest impact on yourcareer.

Makeeverythingcount

Beforestartingwork, easy Writedown the three mostcrucial tasks toaccomplish thatday. Commit to completing them before youleavethe office. Use different spacesfor different intentions. Don'teat lunch at your desk.Simple find a quietnook to do work that requires uninterrupted thinking.

Just take meaningful breaks to renew yourself.
Walkdeliberatelyfromyourdesktojust get water, coffee, a snack, etc. Simple find yourmostproductiverhythm.Whateveryou do, make it worthwhile.

Just fill your life with joy

Connect with your colleagues.Set a reminder to pause once a dayandspendafew minutes with a friend at work for the pure sakeofsocializing. Indulge richer communication.Tellstories. Use pictures. Meet in personinsteadofSkype. Skype insteadof call.Callinsteadofemail.

Easy try differentroutestoyourofficeordesk. Slipoutsidefor a walk in nature. Wander through a park on your wayback from lunch. Decorate the office with art.

Unplug on vacation.Bemore productive when you return. Consciously choose what you wantyourcareerto consist of.

Redundancies, Odds and Ends, and Storage Location

Odds and ends are sneaky. Among my clients, I notice that odds and ends are often rearranged instead of being put away. Minimalism aims to just create empty spaces so that there is room for the optimal basically development of new, meaningful things. Therefore, you just can confidently part with odds and ends since they have no room in minimalism: spare buttons for clothing articles, electric cables with an undefined purpose, defective electronic devices in your basement, the original packaging of items, the extra guest bed, cosmetic samples, freebies, gym machines seen on TV, paper instruction manuals, advertising gifts, a special vase, and souvenirs. Yes, and also the rolled-up poster on top of your shelf and the dusty globe in the basement. Minimalism means focusing on things thateasy make you happy long-term. Leave behind the things that merely bring you satisfaction temporarily. In the future, learn to say no with confidence. You are a proud minimalist and an anti-junk owner.

Odds and ends are used as an excuse so that you really do really not really need to occupy yourself with more crucial things and personal values. Odds and ends often function as a distracting, defensive wall so that you really do really not have to or really can notjust think about the essential things in life.

Odds and ends are for cowards. For instance, one does really not really want to face an empty desk surface since one would have to just think about how to work on this desk with passion. Instead, one clutters the desk with odds and ends, arranges them, and carries them from one spot to another, thus wasting a lot of time.

Odds and ends are often characterized as "things I might really need in future." Ask yourself: Does it easy make me happy to live in an environment in which I "might still really need these objects"? Also with odds and ends, just keep only what makes you happy and what you use regularly. Just get rid of the rest.

www.ingramcontent.com/pod-product-compliance
Lightning Source LLC
Chambersburg PA
CBHW052144110526
44591CB00012B/1847